JUSTIN DELLO JOIO
SONATA FOR PIANO

1. Theme and Variations

2. Romance

3. Finale Fantasia

Revised in September 2005

Recorded by pianist Garrick Ohlsson, on Bridge Records (CD #9220)

Cover drawing by Andrew DeVries

ISBN 978-1-4950-1893-0

EDWARD B. MARKS MUSIC COMPANY

EXCLUSIVELY DISTRIBUTED BY

HAL•LEONARD® CORPORATION

7777 W. BLUEMOUND RD. P.O. BOX 13819 MILWAUKEE, WI 53213

www.ebmarks.com
www.halleonard.com

PERFORMANCE NOTES

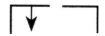

This symbol is occasionally employed to specify the principal voice which must be brought out accordingly.

This symbol denotes a free accelerando within the specified time duration.

to Vincent Persichetti

Sonata for Piano

1. Theme and Variations

JUSTIN DELLO JOIO

Duration: c. 25`

4

VARIATION 1

VARIATION 2

Vivace scherzevole, umoristico (♩ = c. 92-96)

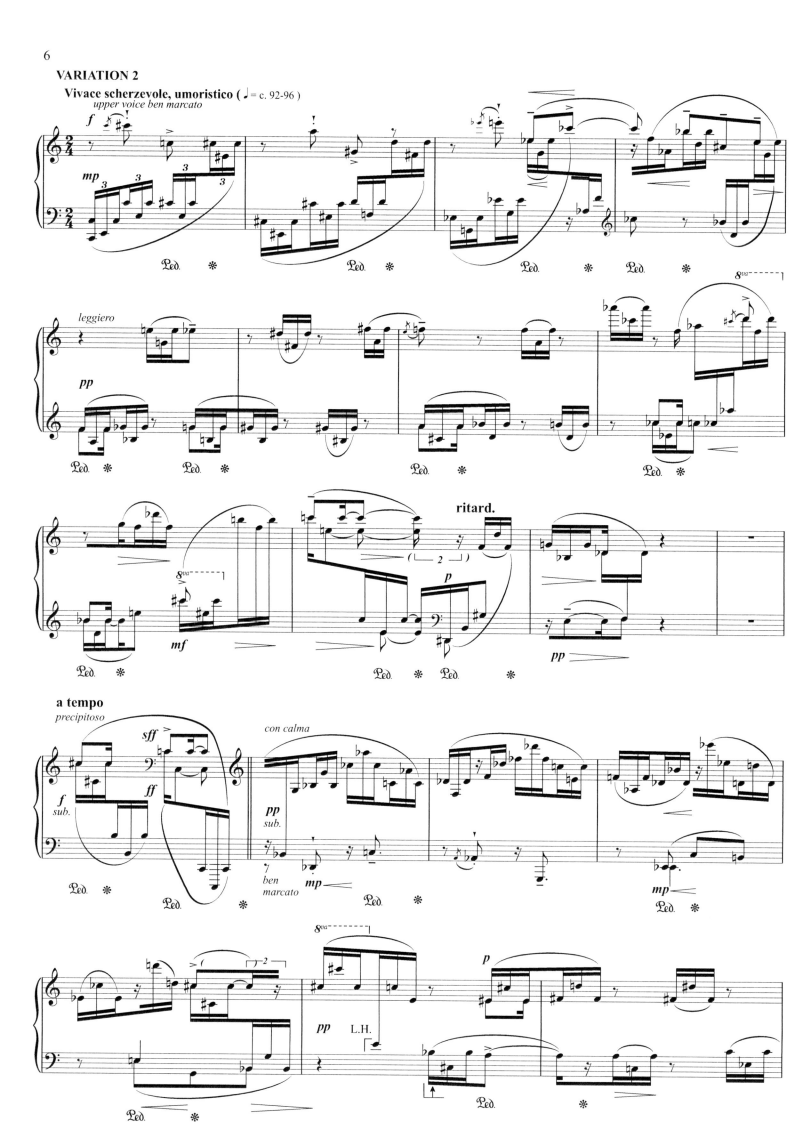

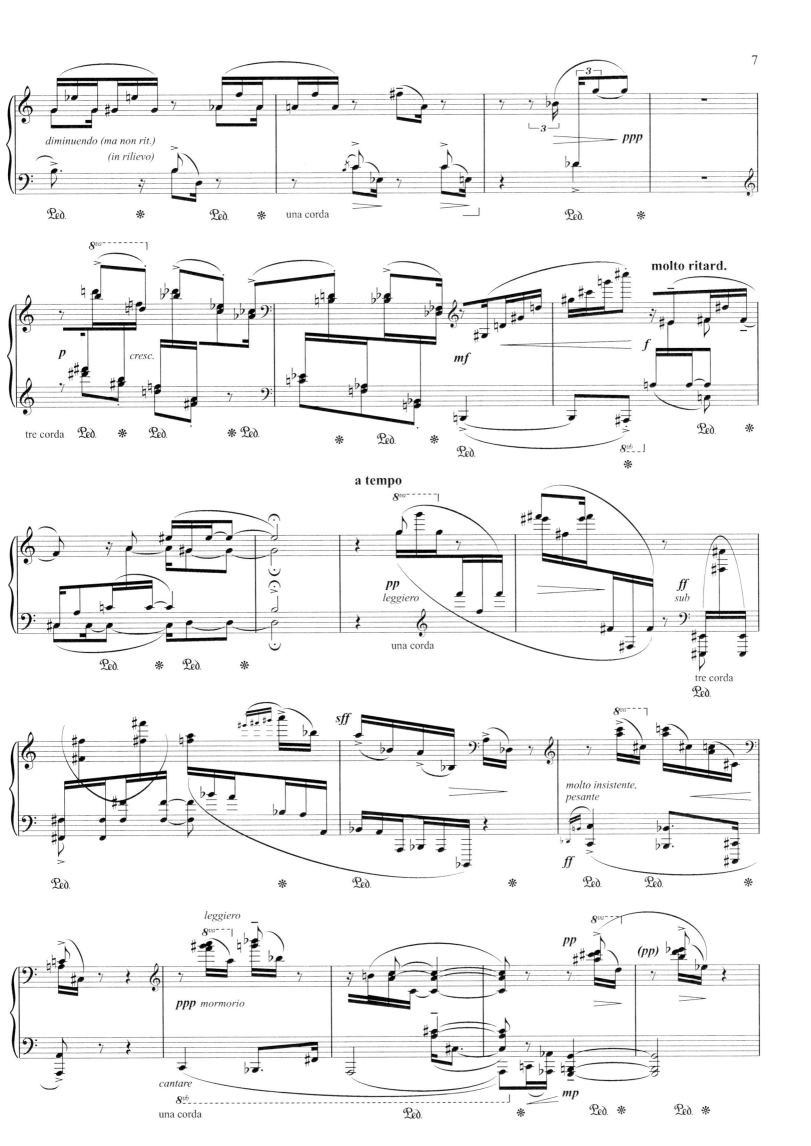

VARIATION 3
Andante grazioso (♩ = c. 54)
molto legato ed espressivo

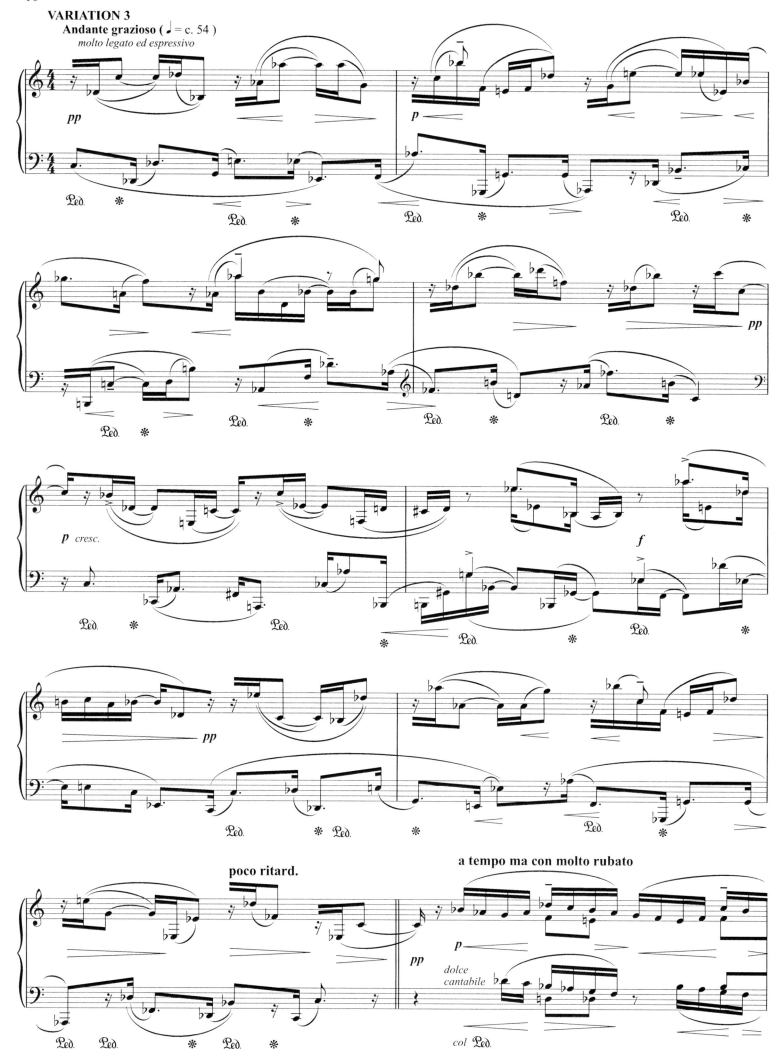

VARIATION 4

Vivace con fuoco (♩ = c. 132-138)

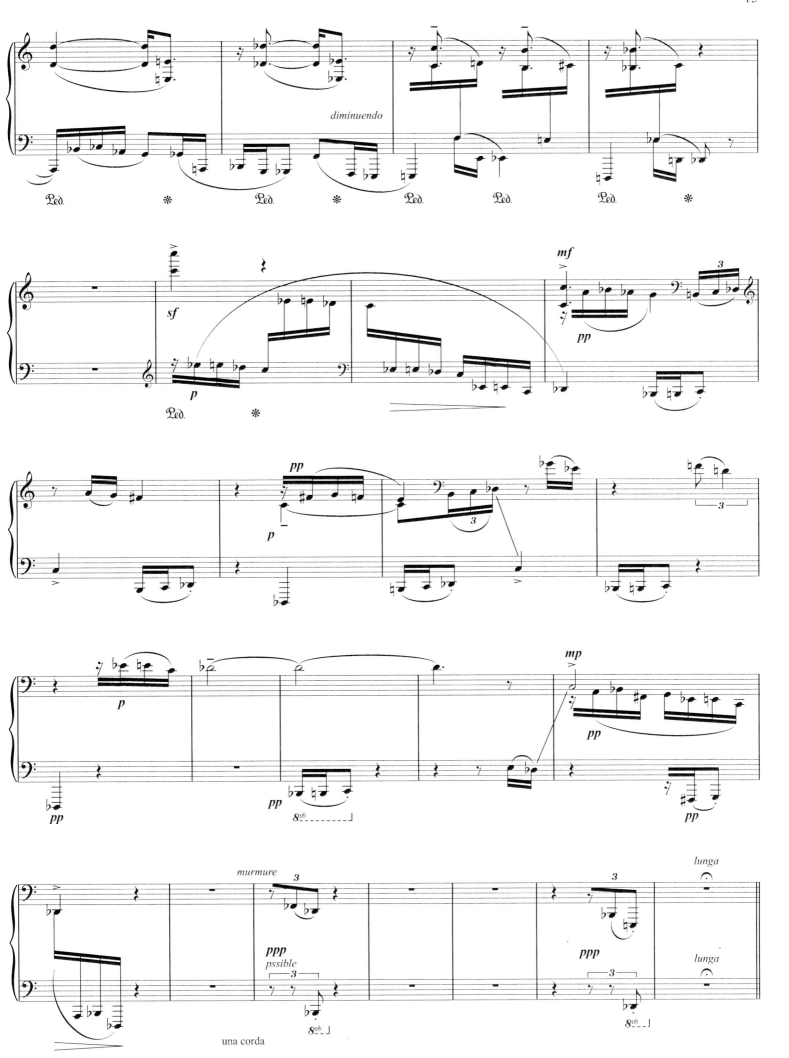

VARIATION 5
Lento molto intensamente (♩ = c. 42)

NOTE: All trills and tremolo are played one dynamic level softer than the other voices

Movendo (♩ = c. 46)

Tempo I
Maestoso sonoro (♩ = c. 42)

Movendo, piú mosso (♩ = c. 66)

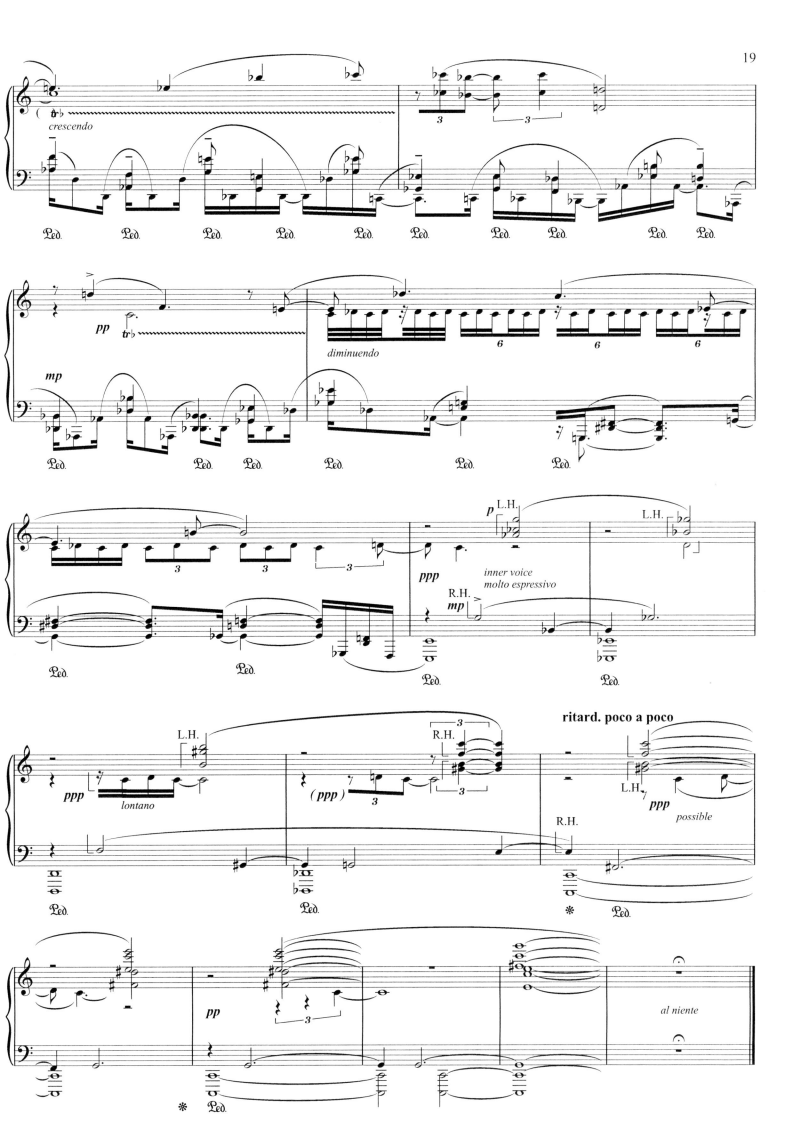

2. Romance

Tempo I (♩ = c. 60)

cantabile

Poco meno mosso (♩ = c. 52)

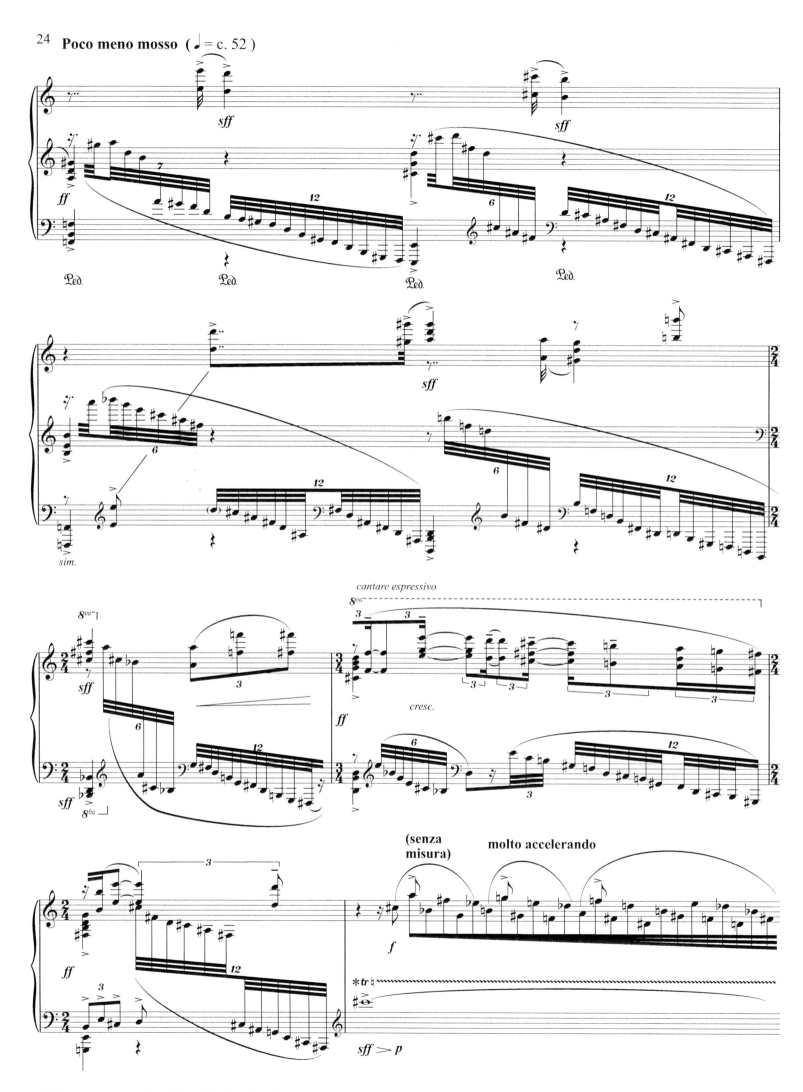

*Right hand may start the trill, with left hand taking over as soon as conveniently possible

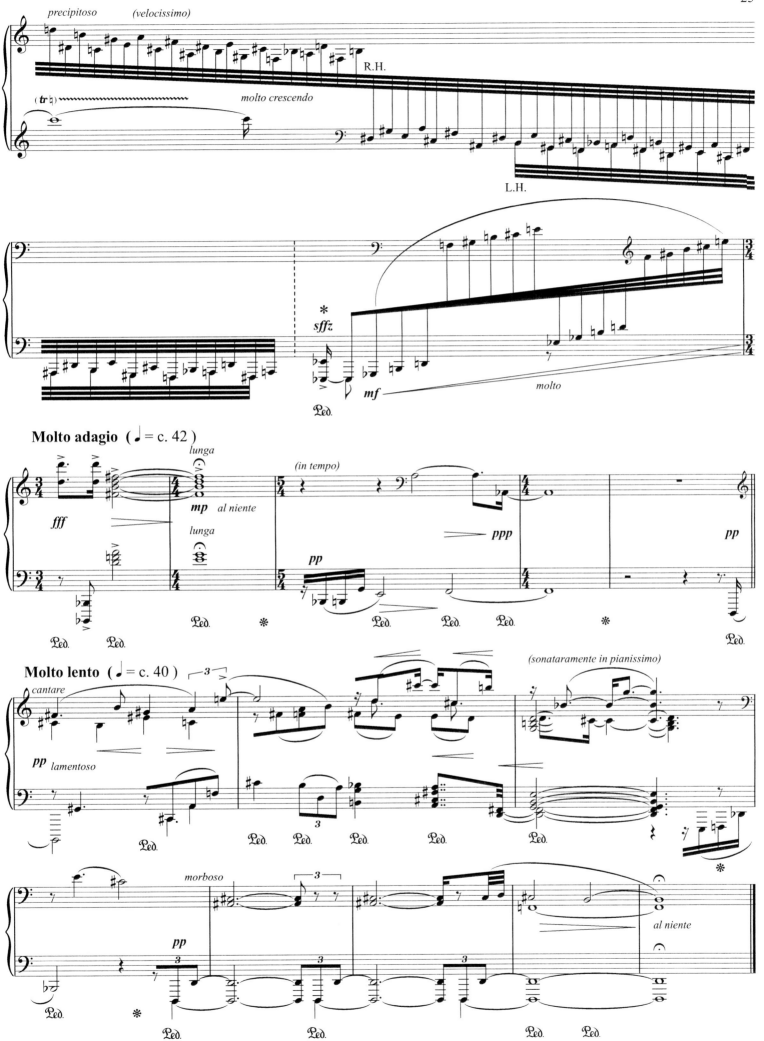

*Performer using an extended-range Bosëndorfer double the E ♭ an octave lower.

3. Finale Fantasia

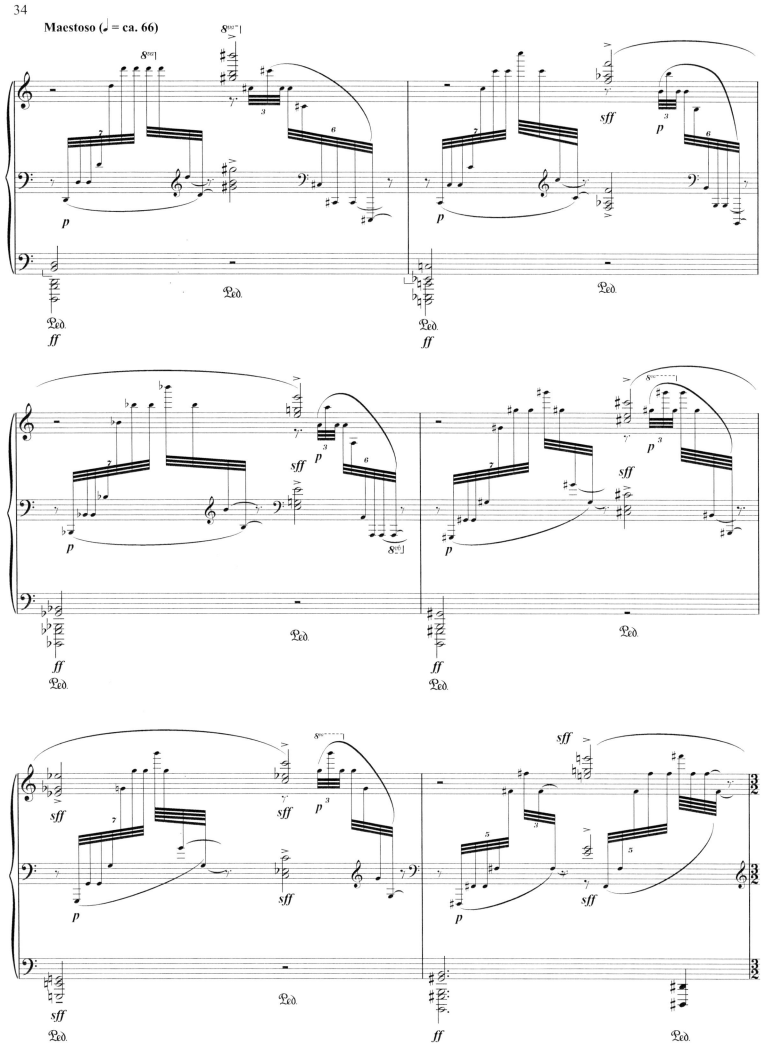

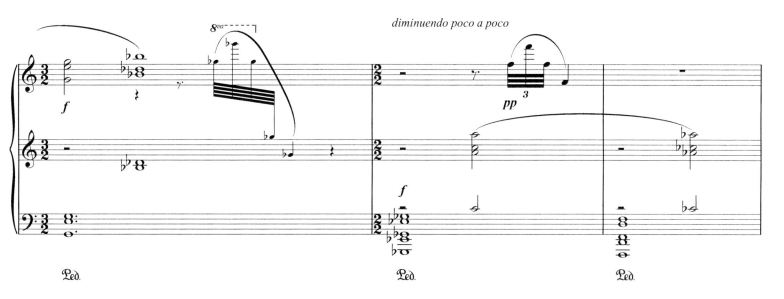

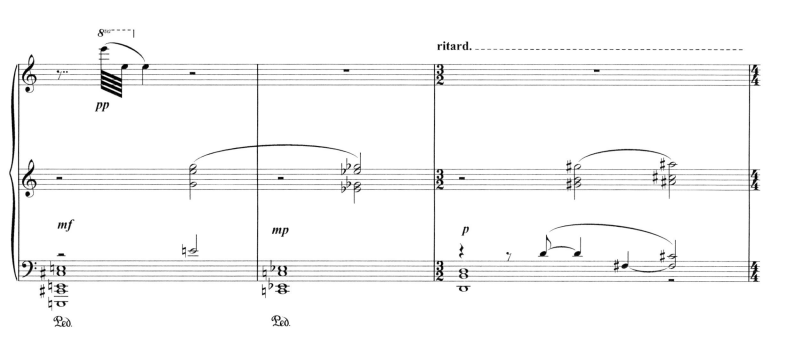

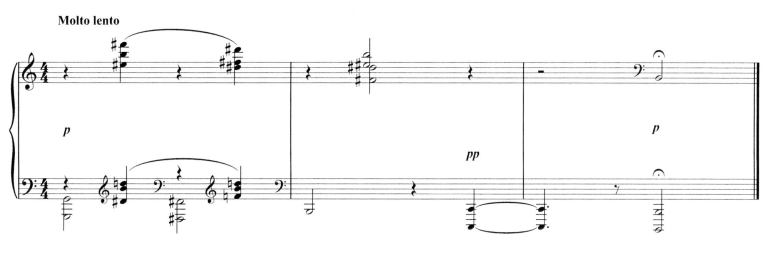